Scripture Anchor

"Do not be conformed to this world but be transformed by the renewing of your mind."
— Romans 12:2

Renewal is practiced.
Transformation is intentional.
Truth changes everything.

This Book Is Gifted With Love

This devotional was given to:

____

From:

____

A special message:

____

____

____

____

____

Date:

____

Contents

A Note on Being Trauma-Informed (Read This First)

This devotional was written for people who have survived things that changed them.

Not people who have it all together. Not people who have finished healing. But people still in the middle of it, who some days feel steady and other days feel like the ground is shifting beneath them again. If that is you, you are exactly who this book is for.

Trauma-informed simply means this: you will not be pushed here. You will not be shamed for where you are. You will not be handed a timeline or told that faith requires you to feel differently than you actually feel right now.

Before you go any further, hold these truths:

You do not have to revisit details that do not feel safe. You do not have to push through emotions to prove your faith is real. You do not have to force forgiveness, manufacture peace, or rush reconciliation to demonstrate that healing is happening. And if something in these pages surfaces more than you can carry alone, you are strongly encouraged to seek support. A counselor, a therapist, a trusted pastor, a safe friend. Healing was never meant to happen in isolation.

Here is what trauma does, and what it does not do.

It impacts the nervous system. It shapes survival thinking. It teaches the body to brace, to anticipate, to stay alert long past the point when alertness is necessary. Your body may have learned hypervigilance. Your mind may scan for danger before deciding it is safe to rest. Your heart may still flinch at things that would not register for someone with a different history.

None of that means you are defective. It means you adapted to survive. Those adaptations were not failures, they were intelligent responses to real circumstances. They kept you here. But they were never meant to be permanent, and they were never meant to become your identity.

That is what the next 30 days are for.

Not to rush you. Not to force you. Not to demand that you arrive somewhere before you are ready. But to walk steadily, truth by truth, toward the person God has been forming all along, the one who has always been beneath the survival, waiting for enough safety to emerge.

God is not in a hurry with your healing. He is not disappointed in your pace. He is not checking a calendar.

He is simply here. And so are you. That is enough to begin.

INTRODUCTION: Renewing Your Mind, One Truth at a Time

If you are holding this book, you have likely already done something brave. You have acknowledged that something needs to change, that the way things have been running in your mind, your relationships, your sense of self does not have to be permanent.

That acknowledgment is not small. For many people, it takes years.

Trauma trains the mind to stay alert, guarded, braced. That wiring may have kept you alive, but it does not have to run your life forever. Romans 12:2 tells us we are transformed by the renewing of our minds, not by pretending the pain is not real, not by minimizing what happened, not by spiritually bypassing the grief that deserves space, but by steadily and deliberately replacing the lies that feel like facts with what God actually says.

That is what this journey is built around.

Every day follows the same rhythm, because renewal requires repetition, not novelty. You will name a lie. You will replace it with truth rooted in Scripture. And you will practice embodying that truth in one small, concrete way before the day is over. Not perfectly. Not dramatically. Just honestly, and as consistently as you can.

Renewal is not theoretical. It is practiced. It is the accumulated weight of small decisions made over time, the choice, again and again, to test the loudest thought in your head against what God says and to trust His answer more than your fear.

This journey moves in a deliberate direction. The first week creates safety, naming patterns, understanding the wiring, establishing the foundation everything else will be built on. The second week rebuilds identity, who you are, who you belong to, what you are and are not defined by. The third week reclaims strength, the kind that is honest about weakness and rooted in something steadier than performance. And the final week moves toward purpose, because healing that stays only with you was never the full intention.

God restores survivors. Then He raises leaders.

You do not have to believe every truth perfectly for it to begin working. You do not have to feel ready, feel strong, or feel like someone who deserves 30 days of this kind of attention. You only have to be willing to show up and tell the truth.

That is the only requirement.

You are not behind. You are not broken. You are not alone. And you are more ready than you think.

DAY 1
I Renounce the Lie

The Lie

"This is just how I am now."

Somewhere along the way, a thought settled in and stopped being questioned. Old patterns, the familiar ones, the worn grooves of the mind, kept running because no one told them to stop. They felt too much like home to challenge.

The Truth in Christ

"Be transformed by the renewing of your mind."

In Christ, no one is stuck with old wiring. The mind can be renewed, gently, steadily, truth by truth.

Scripture Anchor

Romans 12:2

Devotional

Today is not about pretending the pain isn't real. It is about deciding that the pain does not get the final word.

For a long time, the lies felt like facts. They sounded reasonable. Protective. Even wise. That is what trauma does, it makes survival thinking feel like identity. Hypervigilance begins to feel like personality. Guardedness gets mistaken for maturity. Bracing becomes a way of life.

But survival patterns are not the same as truth.

Living inside those patterns long enough teaches you something: just because something kept you safe once does not mean it gets to lead you forever. Your nervous system learned to brace. Your mind learned to anticipate danger. Those were good and necessary adaptations, for a season. But God offers something new: the ability to discern instead of fear. To pause instead of spiral. To respond instead of react.

Renewal is not dramatic. It is deliberate.

It begins not with a feeling, but with a decision, one small, courageous choice: I will not automatically agree with the loudest thought in my head. I will test it against truth.

Transformation does not wait for you to feel different. It begins the moment you choose differently.

Renounce + Receive

I renounce: "This is just who I am now."
I receive: "God is renewing my mind, one thought at a time."

Daily Affirmation

I am being transformed by truth.

Prayer

Jesus, teach me to recognize the lies that feel normal, the ones that have been there so long I stopped noticing them. Slow me down enough to question them. Renew my mind with what is steady, clean, and true. Amen.

Action Step

Write down one recurring thought you have had lately. Ask: "Is this truth, or is this trauma?" Replace it with one sentence of Scripture.

DAY 2
I Am Not My Past

The Lie
"My past disqualifies me."

Shame has a way of following you into rooms you were meant to lead in, even after healing begins, even after your choices change. The past can feel like a permanent credential, just not the kind you want.

The Truth in Christ
"If anyone is in Christ, they are a new creation."

In Christ, you are redeemed, not reduced to what you survived.

Scripture Anchor
2 Corinthians 5:17

Devotional
Shame and humility are not the same thing, but trauma can make them feel identical.

Humility says: I needed God, and He came.
Shame says: You are what happened to you.

One moves you forward. The other keeps you small.

There is a quiet lie that can settle in even after healing begins, the idea that carrying your past like a weight is somehow spiritual. That rehearsing your failures keeps you humble. That the rooms you are called to stand in were meant for someone with a cleaner story.

But that is not humility. That is shame in disguise.

Redemption is not denial. God does not erase history, He transforms what it means. He takes what tried to destroy you and weaves it into wisdom, compassion, and discernment. The very things you survived become the very things that make you trustworthy to someone still in the middle of it.

Your past is part of your testimony. It is not your identity.

The choices made in survival mode do not get to define who you are becoming in freedom. Today, you do not have to disqualify what God has already qualified.

Renounce + Receive

I renounce: "My past disqualifies me."
I receive: "In Christ, I am redeemed and made new."

Daily Affirmation

I am not my past. I am redeemed.

Prayer

God, untangle shame from my story. Help me see my past through the lens of redemption, not regret. Give me the courage to stand in the rooms You've called me to, without shrinking. Amen.

Action Step

Write this sentence somewhere you will see it today: "My past is part of my story, not my identity." Read it out loud. Mean it a little more than yesterday.

DAY 3
I Am Worthy of Love

The Lie
"I'm not worthy of love."

When love has been withheld, made conditional, or used as leverage, something quietly shifts. You stop expecting it to stay. You learn to take what is offered and call it enough, even when it is not.

The Truth in Christ
"We love because He first loved us."

In Christ, you are deeply loved, before you perform, before you prove, before you perfect.

Scripture Anchor
1 John 4:19

Devotional
When love has been inconsistent, your body remembers. You may smile on the outside and brace on the inside. You may long for connection and expect disappointment just as strongly.

That is not weakness. That is wisdom shaped by experience.

But here is what God's love refuses to do: it does not withdraw affection to teach lessons. It does not use silence to control. It does not require performance before offering presence. It does not leave because you were too much, or stay only because you made yourself small enough.

Human love can wound in all of those ways. God's love cannot, because it is not sourced in the same place.

Healing in this area is often slow. Learning to receive love without scanning it for a catch, without waiting for it to expire, without wondering what it will cost you, takes time. If receiving love still feels unfamiliar or even unsafe, you are not broken. You are retraining a nervous system that learned to protect itself. That is not a flaw. That is evidence of survival.

You are no longer measuring your worth by who stayed. You are learning to measure it by who chose you first.

Renounce + Receive
I renounce: "I'm not worthy of love."
I receive: "I am fully and freely loved by God."

Daily Affirmation
I am worthy of love because I belong to God.

Prayer
Father, heal the places in me where love felt unsafe. Teach me what steady, consistent love truly looks like. Help me receive Yours without flinching and without waiting for it to disappear. Amen.

Action Step
Place your hand over your heart. Say out loud: "God's love is steady over me." If it feels awkward, say it anyway. Your nervous system is listening.

DAY 4
I Am Enough Because Christ Is

The Lie
"I'm not enough."

It shows up quietly at first, working a little harder, explaining a little more, making yourself a little more useful than necessary. Until one day, you realize you have built your entire sense of safety around never being caught falling short.

The Truth in Christ
"My grace is sufficient for you."

In Christ, you are enough, not because of your performance, but because of His sufficiency.

Scripture Anchor
2 Corinthians 12:9

Devotional
Striving can look spiritual. Productivity can look responsible. Over functioning can look strong.

But underneath it all is often something more tender, the fear of being overlooked, rejected, or replaced the moment you stop being useful.

You may know what it is like to make yourself indispensable. To anticipate needs before they are spoken. To stay one step ahead of disappointment by giving people no reason to leave. It feels responsible. It can even feel like love.

But exhaustion is not holiness. And performing for belonging is not the same as being in relationship.

God never asked you to become superhuman to deserve love. His grace fills what you lack, and that is not failure. That is design. You were never meant to be enough on your own. Christ is the Savior. The position is filled.

If you slow down today and anxiety rises, pay attention to that. It does not mean you are lazy. It may mean your body is detoxing from striving, learning, perhaps for the first time, that rest is not a threat.

You are allowed to be human. That was always the plan.

Renounce + Receive

I renounce: "I am not enough."
I receive: "Christ is sufficient in me."

Daily Affirmation

I am enough because Christ is enough.

Prayer

Jesus, release me from the exhausting work of proving myself. Teach me to rest without the guilt that says I should be doing more. Anchor my worth in Your sufficiency, not my output. Amen.

Action Step

Do one thing today at 80% effort instead of 110%. Notice what comes up when you do not go all the way, without judging what you find. Whatever surfaces is information, not indictment.

DAY 5
I Am Not Broken — I Am Healing

The Lie
"Something is wrong with me."

It is the conclusion that forms when your reactions feel too big, too sudden, or too hard to explain. When you shut down in moments you wish you had stayed open. When anxiety shows up uninvited and you spend more energy judging it than understanding it.

The Truth in Christ
"The Lord is close to the brokenhearted."

In Christ, you are not defective, you are healing.

Scripture Anchor
Psalm 34:18

Devotional
For a long time, it is easy to mistake trauma responses for character flaws.

Anxiety gets labeled dramatic. Shutting down gets called cold. Needing reassurance becomes too much. The very responses that once kept you safe are reframed as evidence that something in you is fundamentally wrong.

But trauma responses are adaptations, not indictments.

Your nervous system did exactly what it was designed to do. It learned the terrain. It mapped the danger. It built systems to protect you when protection was necessary. That is not weakness. That is not dysfunction. That is a body that fought to keep you alive.

God is not standing over that process with disappointment. He is near to it. Close to it. Present in it.

Healing begins to look different when you trade criticism for curiosity. When the question shifts from "What is wrong with me?" to "What is this reaction trying to protect?" That single shift changes everything, because you stop treating yourself like a problem to be solved and start treating yourself like a person being restored.

That is what God has been doing all along.

Renounce + Receive
I renounce: "Something is wrong with me."
I receive: "God is healing me with patience and care."

Daily Affirmation
I am not broken. I am healing.

Prayer
God, soften the self-judgment I have carried for so long. Help me extend to myself the same compassion You have never stopped showing me. Restore what survival had to protect, gently and in Your time. Amen.

Action Step
The next time you feel triggered, pause before the self-criticism begins. Say out loud: "My body is trying to protect me. I am safe right now." Then take one slow breath and mean it as much as you can.

DAY 6
God Has Not Rejected Me

The Lie

"God has turned away from me."

It is the interpretation that forms in the silence, when prayers feel like they are hitting the ceiling. When struggle follows struggle, and the distance begins to feel less like a season and more like a sentence.

The Truth in Christ

"I will never leave you nor forsake you."

In Christ, you are not abandoned, you are held. God's presence is not fragile. His love does not withdraw when you are overwhelmed.

Scripture Anchor

Hebrews 13:5

Devotional

Rejection leaves an imprint that does not stay neatly in the past.

It travels with you. It shows up in the way your body tenses when someone goes quiet. In the way delay begins to feel like dismissal. In the way struggle starts to feel like punishment. If your history includes people who left without warning, who withheld presence to punish, or who disappeared when you needed them most, your nervous system learned a very specific lesson: silence means something is wrong.

That lesson does not automatically unlearn itself when you come to God.

But here is what God does not do. He does not pull away when you struggle. He does not grow tired of your process. He does not withhold presence to teach you a lesson. He does not go quiet because He is disappointed.

There is a critical difference between God feeling distant and God being absent, and your nervous system may not know the difference yet. That is not a failure of faith. That is a wound still healing.

Scripture does not fluctuate with your nervous system. God's faithfulness is not mood-based. His covenant is not fragile. His presence is not conditional on your ability to feel it.

You are learning to live in the space between feeling and fact. When anxiety rises and whispers, "He left," you answer with what He said: He said He would not.

That is not denial. That is faith doing its quiet, steady work.

Renounce + Receive

I renounce: "God has rejected me."

I receive: "God is faithful, present, and steady with me."

Daily Affirmation

I am not abandoned. God is with me, even when I cannot feel Him.

Prayer

Lord, heal the places in me where silence feels like rejection. Anchor me in Your presence that does not move, even when my feelings say otherwise. Teach my body, slowly and gently, what Your faithfulness actually feels like. Amen.

Action Step

Write this somewhere you will see it today: "God feeling quiet is not God being gone." Read it aloud once, then let it sit with you longer than feels comfortable.

DAY 7
I Am Not Alone

The Lie

"I have to do this alone."

It started as survival. Needing no one meant no one could let you down. Carrying everything yourself meant nothing could be dropped on you. Independence felt like the safest thing you had built, until it began to feel like a prison.

The Truth in Christ

"God sets the lonely in families."

In Christ, you are not designed for isolation. Safe connection is not a luxury, it is part of your healing.

Scripture Anchor

Psalm 68:6

Devotional

There is a version of strength that looks impressive from the outside and feels like slow suffocation from the inside.

You handle everything. You ask for nothing. You show up for everyone and quietly fall apart alone. And when someone offers help, you deflect, because accepting it would mean admitting you needed it, and needing things has not always been safe.

Hyper-independence is one of trauma's most convincing disguises. It presents itself as maturity. As resilience. As not being a burden. But underneath it is often a nervous system that learned a painful lesson: people leave, disappoint, or weaponize what you share. So you stopped sharing. You stopped leaning. You stopped asking.

But isolation was never the design.

Even Jesus, fully God and fully capable of handling everything alone, chose community. He invited friends into His process. He asked them to stay awake with Him in the garden. He wept with people before He performed miracles. If the Son of God did not do this alone, you do not have to either.

Connection does not require instant trust. It requires one small, wise step toward one safe person. If that feels terrifying, that is understandable. Your body remembers what happened the last time you leaned. But healing asks you to try again, slowly, carefully, and with discernment.

Not because you are weak, but because you are healing.

Renounce + Receive

I renounce: "I have to do everything alone."

I receive: "God is placing safe support around me."

Daily Affirmation

I am supported. I am not alone.

Prayer

God, heal the part of me that decided it was safer to need no one. Give me the courage to take small steps toward safe connection. Surround me with people who are wise, steady, and trustworthy, and help me recognize them when they show up. Amen.

Action Step

Send one honest message today, even if it is just five words: "I could use some prayer." Let someone in, even just a little. That is not weakness. That is the bravest thing you will do today.

DAY 8
My Pain Is Not My Identity

The Lie

"What happened to me defines me."

It happens so gradually you do not notice it at first. The wound becomes the lens. The experience becomes the explanation. Until one day, you realize the story you tell yourself about who you are begins with what was done to you.

The Truth in Christ

"I have called you by name; you are Mine."

In Christ, you are named by God, not by your trauma.

Scripture Anchor

Isaiah 43:1

Devotional

Pain changes you. That is not up for debate. Trauma leaves impressions, in your body, in your thoughts, in the way you move through rooms and relationships. It would be dishonest to pretend otherwise.

But being changed by something is not the same as being defined by it.

There is a difference between what happened to you and who you are. Trauma works hard to collapse that distinction. Your brain, in its effort to protect you, links identity and experience together, because if you understand yourself through the lens of what hurt you, you can anticipate it next time. It is a survival strategy dressed up as self-knowledge.

But God never introduced you by your wounds.

He does not call you by what you survived. He does not lead with your worst moment or your hardest season. He calls you daughter. He calls you chosen. He calls you His. These are not titles you earn after you have healed enough, they are names He gave before you had anything to prove.

Untangling identity from experience takes time and gentleness. If it feels difficult to separate who you are from what happened, that is not a sign you are doing it wrong. It is a sign the work is real and worth doing.

Today, you practice a new introduction, one that begins with what God says, not what pain wrote.

Renounce + Receive

I renounce: "My trauma defines me."
I receive: "God defines who I am."

Daily Affirmation

I am more than what I have survived.

Prayer

Father, untangle my identity from my pain. Where the two have been fused for so long I cannot tell them apart, bring Your light and Your gentleness. Teach me to see myself the way You do. Remind me of my true name. Amen.

Action Step

Write your name at the top of a blank page. Under it, write three identity truths God speaks over you, not three wounds, not three things you have survived. Just three things He calls you. Start there. That is your true introduction.

DAY 9
I Can Be Safe and Still Be Strong

The Lie
"If I let my guard down, I will get hurt."

So the guard stays up, in every room, with every person. Even the safe ones. Even on quiet Tuesday afternoons when nothing is wrong, the body does not know that yet, so it stays ready anyway.

The Truth in Christ
"God is our refuge and strength."

In Christ, safety and strength are not opposites. You do not have to choose between them.

Scripture Anchor
Psalm 46:1

Devotional
Chronic vigilance has a way of disguising itself as competence.

Being the one who anticipates everything feels responsible. Staying one step ahead of potential harm feels wise. Keeping your guard up feels like strength, until you realize you cannot remember the last time your shoulders were not somewhere near your ears.

Jaw clenched. Breath shallow. Body braced. Not because anything is wrong in this moment, but because your nervous system stopped waiting for confirmation. It decided long ago that staying ready was safer than being caught off guard. And for a season, it was right.

But chronic tension is not strength. It is fatigue wearing strength's clothes.

God as refuge means something significant: you do not have to be your own full-time protector. That role was never meant to be yours alone. He does not shame the caution your body learned, He understands exactly where it came from. But He also does not want you standing guard over your own life indefinitely, never resting, never releasing, never allowing anything to feel safe enough to exhale.

Safety is not naivety. Relaxing is not the same as being careless. Letting one muscle soften does not mean the walls come down forever, it means you are learning, slowly, that not every moment requires defense.

Today, strength looks quieter than usual. Today, strength looks like one slow breath.

Renounce + Receive

I renounce: "Safety makes me weak."

I receive: "God is my refuge and strength."

Daily Affirmation

I am strong, and I am allowed to feel safe.

Prayer

God, teach my body what safety actually feels like, not as a concept, but as an experience. Help me release the tension that has been working overtime. Be my refuge in the moments when letting go feels like the most frightening thing I could do. Amen.

Action Step

Right now, unclench your jaw. Drop your shoulders if they will let you. Take one breath that goes all the way down. Say quietly: "I am safe in this moment." You do not have to believe it completely yet. Just let your body hear it.

DAY 10
I Don't Have to Earn Love

The Lie

"Love must be earned."

So you learned the math early. Stay useful. Stay needed. Stay one step ahead of disappointment. Make yourself worth keeping, because love, in your experience, was never simply given. It was always exchanged for something.

The Truth in Christ

"God demonstrates His love for us in this: while we were still sinners, Christ died for us."

In Christ, you are loved before you perform. The work was finished before you had anything to offer.

Scripture Anchor

Romans 5:8

Devotional

Conditional love is an exhausting teacher.

It trains you to scan every room for signs of approval. To read faces for early warning signals. To adjust, shrink, overextend, or perform, whatever the moment requires to keep love from walking out the door. It can feel like attentiveness. It can look like effort. But underneath it, fear is doing the work love was always meant to do.

You may know what it is like to make yourself indispensable. To give more than you have so no one has a reason to leave. To feel the quiet panic that rises when you stop being useful, as if the moment you stop producing, you stop mattering.

That is not a character flaw. It is a wound shaped by conditional love.

But God did not wait for you to be ready. He did not wait for you to heal, mature, perform, or prove yourself worthy. He went first, before you cleaned anything up, before you had anything to show. If love had to be earned, Christ would not have gone to the cross for someone who had not yet become deserving. But He did. Which means the love was never about earning.

Unlearning the reflex to prove your worth is slow work. If anxiety rises when you stop performing, that makes sense. Your system learned that usefulness equals safety. But you are not a transaction. You are not a service. You are someone God loved on purpose, before you had anything to give.

Today, you receive instead of chase.

Renounce + Receive
I renounce: "I must earn love."
I receive: "God loves me freely and fully."

Daily Affirmation
I am loved without striving.

Prayer
Father, break the cycle of performance that has lived in me for so long it feels like personality. Teach me to receive love without immediately looking for what it will cost me. Anchor my worth in Your finished work, not my ongoing effort. Amen.

Action Step

When someone thanks you or compliments you today, resist the reflex to deflect or downplay it. Simply say, "Thank you." No disclaimers. No redirecting. Let the kindness land. That is practice. That is enough.

DAY 11
My Voice Matters

The Lie

"Speaking up is dangerous."

So you learned to edit before you spoke. To weigh every word against the cost of saying it. To make yourself quieter, smaller, easier, until silence became so automatic you stopped noticing you had chosen it.

The Truth in Christ

"The righteous cry out, and the Lord hears them."

In Christ, your voice is not a threat, it is heard. God does not flinch when you speak.

Scripture Anchor

Psalm 34:17

Devotional

Silence can be a survival strategy so effective you forget it was ever a choice.

There are environments where speaking truth carries consequences. Where honesty is punished. Where clarity is labeled as aggression and questions are treated as rebellion. If you grew up in those environments, or spent years within them, your nervous system learned the lesson well: stay quiet, stay safe.

But survival silence is not a lifelong calling.

The editing, the minimizing, the swallowing of sentences halfway through, these were adaptations. Intelligent ones, even. They protected you when protection was necessary. But they were never meant to be permanent. They were never meant to become your personality.

God is not intimidated by your questions. He is not threatened by your honesty. He does not withdraw when you speak clearly, push back, or say the thing you have been holding for years. He is not one of the people who punished you for having a voice. That distinction matters more than it might feel right now.

Learning to speak again is slow work. If your body tightens at the thought of confrontation, that makes sense, your nervous system is consulting its records, and the records say speaking up has costs. But those records are being updated, slowly, entry by entry.

Today, using your voice does not mean being loud. It may mean saying one honest sentence. It may mean staying present in the room instead of going quiet. It may mean praying out loud for the first time in years.

Your voice matters, not because of its volume, but because it is yours.

Renounce + Receive

I renounce: "My voice doesn't matter."
I receive: "God hears me, and I am learning to speak."

Daily Affirmation

My voice matters to God.

Prayer

Lord, heal the fear that wrapped itself around my voice and called it wisdom. Give me the courage to speak with clarity, not perfectly, but honestly. Teach me to use my voice in a way that is steady, true, and unafraid. Amen.

Action Step

Say one small truth today that you would normally swallow. It does not have to be big. It does not have to be confrontational. It simply has to be honest. That counts. That is your voice finding its way back.

DAY 12
Boundaries Are Holy

The Lie

"Boundaries are selfish."

So you absorbed what should have been deflected. You said yes when everything in you said no. You gave past empty and called it love, because somewhere along the way you learned that unlimited availability was the most spiritual thing you could offer.

The Truth in Christ

Jesus modeled boundaries.

In Christ, boundaries are not rejection, they are stewardship. Protecting what God is restoring is not selfishness. It is wisdom.

Scripture Anchor

Mark 1:35–38

Devotional

There is a version of love that has been confused with self-erasure for far too long.

If someone needed you, you showed up. If pressure came, you absorbed it. If saying no created tension, you said yes and managed the discomfort privately. You told yourself it was Christlike. You told yourself unlimited availability was the mark of genuine love.

But exhaustion is not holiness. And self-abandonment is not sanctification.

Look at what Jesus did in Mark 1. He had just healed many, real people with real needs, and He had met them. But when morning came, He withdrew. He went to a solitary place to pray. And when His disciples found Him with urgency, "Everyone is looking for you," He did not immediately return. He chose where to go next based on His calling, not the crowd's expectations.

Jesus did not allow urgency to dictate obedience.

That moment reframes everything. If the Son of God, fully capable of healing every person in every town, chose to withdraw, chose to protect the source, then boundaries are not a failure of love. They are an act of wisdom that makes sustained love possible.

Boundaries are not walls built from bitterness. They are fences built from wisdom. They protect calling, capacity, peace, and the healing God is doing in you, the kind that requires space and safety to take root.

If guilt rises when you say no, that makes sense. Many people were conditioned to equate self-sacrifice with spirituality so thoroughly that limits feel like sin. But God does not ask you to erase yourself to prove love. He asks you to steward what He is rebuilding.

Today, stewardship wins over people-pleasing.

Renounce + Receive

I renounce: "Boundaries are selfish."

I receive: "Boundaries are wise and God-honoring."

Daily Affirmation

My boundaries protect what God is rebuilding in me.

Prayer

Jesus, teach me to love without losing myself in the process. Give me the courage to say yes with peace and no without guilt. Help me steward my healing the way You stewarded Yours, wisely, intentionally, and without apology. Amen.

Action Step

Practice this sentence today, out loud, even if only alone in your car or your kitchen: "That doesn't work for me." Say it until it stops feeling selfish. Because it was never selfish. It was simply new.

DAY 13
I Am Not Too Much

The Lie
"I'm too much."

So you learned to take up less space. To turn down the volume on your emotions, your opinions, your presence. To apologize for the parts of you that felt too large for the rooms you were in, until making yourself smaller became second nature.

The Truth in Christ
"I praise You because I am fearfully and wonderfully made."

In Christ, you are intentionally created, not excessive, not accidental, not a design flaw in need of correction.

Scripture Anchor
Psalm 139:14

Devotional
There is a particular kind of wound that comes from being told, directly or indirectly, that the way you are is simply too much.

Your emotions were labeled dramatic. Your needs were called inconvenient. Your intensity made people uncomfortable, and somehow the responsibility for that discomfort landed on you. So you adapted. You lowered your voice. You softened your convictions. You reduced your enthusiasm to a level that felt more acceptable to the people around you.

But shrinking never brought peace. It only created disconnection, from others, and quietly, from yourself.

Sensitivity is not weakness. Passion is not instability. Depth is not danger. These are not character flaws that need managing, they are dimensions of a person God designed with intention. The same intensity that was criticized in unhealthy environments may be the very thing God uses most powerfully in the right ones.

Trauma can amplify emotions, yes. But it can also sharpen discernment. What some people called too much was often awareness they were not equipped to receive. What was labeled intense was frequently conviction they found inconvenient. The problem was not your volume. The problem was the room.

God does not regret the way He made you. He did not step back from the design and wish He had dialed something down. Fearfully and wonderfully is not a polite compliment, it is a declaration about the care and intention that went into every part of you, including the parts that have been called excessive.

Healing includes learning to occupy your life without a running apology for existing in it.

Today, you take up the space God assigned you, without shrinking, without editing, without asking permission.

Renounce + Receive

I renounce: "I am too much."

I receive: "I am intentionally and wonderfully made."

Daily Affirmation

I am not too much. I am designed on purpose.

Prayer

God, untangle shame from my personality, the shame that settled in when someone decided I was more than they could handle. Help me embrace the way You created me, fully and without apology. Teach me to show up completely, without making myself smaller to make others comfortable. Amen.

Action Step

Notice one moment today when you feel the urge to shrink, to soften, edit, or apologize for yourself. Pause. Breathe. Stay present instead of pulling back. You do not have to perform bigness. You simply have to stop disappearing.

DAY 14
I Belong

The Lie

"I don't really belong anywhere."

So you learned to hover at the edges. To arrive but not settle. To participate just enough to seem present while keeping one foot pointed toward the exit, because belonging, in your experience, could be revoked without warning.

The Truth in Christ

"You are no longer strangers... but members of God's household."

In Christ, you are not an outsider looking in. You are family. Not a guest. Not on probation. Family.

Scripture Anchor

Ephesians 2:19

Devotional

Belonging is one of the deepest human needs, and one of the most complicated to receive when rejection has left its mark.

You can be welcomed into a room and still feel like you are visiting. You can be invited, included, embraced, and still find yourself scanning for the moment when people realize you do not quite fit. That quiet, persistent fear that your presence is tolerated rather than wanted is not dramatic. It is a nervous system doing exactly what it was trained to do: anticipate exclusion before it arrives.

Trauma wires the body for rejection in much the same way it wires it for danger, because in certain seasons, rejection was danger. Being cast out meant being unsafe. So the system learned to stay alert, stay provisional, never fully settle anywhere. It was a reasonable response to an unreasonable situation.

But you are not in that situation anymore. And the belonging God offers operates on entirely different terms.

You are not tolerated by Him. You are not conditionally accepted pending future performance. You are chosen, deliberately, specifically, irreversibly. Adopted into a family you did not have to audition for. Grafted in not because you earned a place, but because He made one. Named not as a visitor, but as a member of His household.

That belonging does not have a revocation clause.

It may take time for that truth to travel from your mind to the places in your body that are still bracing for exclusion. That is okay. Belonging does not always feel immediate, sometimes it grows slowly as safety deepens, layer by layer. You do not have to force it, perform it, or prove you deserve it.

You belong to God first. Every other sense of belonging flows from that anchor.

Renounce + Receive

I renounce: "I don't belong."
I receive: "I am part of God's family."

Daily Affirmation

I belong, fully and securely, to God.

Prayer

Father, quiet the fear of exclusion that follows me into rooms where I am genuinely welcome. Root me so deeply in Your family that old anxieties lose their grip. Help me rest in belonging instead of constantly working to maintain it. Amen.

Action Step

When you enter a room today, any room, say this silently before you walk in: "I am allowed to be here." Not as a question. Not as a hope. As a fact. Because it is one.

DAY 15
I Am Not Disqualified

The Lie

"My mistakes cancel my calling."

So you hesitate at the threshold of every open door. You remember where you fell, and the memory feels like evidence, proof that someone like you should not be stepping into spaces like this. So you wait. You shrink back. You let the moment pass and tell yourself it is humility.

The Truth in Christ

"I will restore to you the years..."

In Christ, your failures are not final, they are redeemed. God does not build His Kingdom by discarding the people who needed mercy most.

Scripture Anchor

Joel 2:25

Devotional

Failure has a long echo.

It follows you past the moment of forgiveness, past the season of growth, past the point where everyone else has moved on. You can receive grace intellectually and still feel hesitation rise in your body the moment you consider stepping into something that matters. The memory alone, not the failure itself, just the memory, can feel like a verdict.

And shame is very good at dressing that verdict up as wisdom.

You should be more careful. You should let someone else lead. You should remember what happened last time. It sounds like discernment. It sounds like humility. But there is a difference between genuine wisdom that informs your next step and shame that simply stops you from taking one.

God wastes nothing. That is not a motivational phrase, it is a theological reality. He does not look at the places where you fell and decide you have become unusable. He does not discard people who needed mercy. He restores them. He rebuilds them. He takes what was broken and works it into wisdom so specific, so hard-won, that it cannot be replicated by someone who never had to fight for it.

Disqualification is a shame narrative. It is not a Kingdom one.

The Kingdom has always been built by people with complicated histories. People who failed publicly, who needed second chances, who carried regret into their calling and let God redeem it along the way. Your story is not the exception to that pattern, it is evidence of it.

If hesitation rises in your body when you consider stepping forward, that makes sense. Visibility has felt like vulnerability before. But restoration is not only internal healing, it also includes reclaiming the ground shame told you to abandon.

Today, you do not shrink back from what God is rebuilding in you.

Renounce + Receive

I renounce: "I am disqualified."

I receive: "God restores and redeems my story."

Daily Affirmation

I am restored, not rejected.

Prayer

God, redeem the places where I fell, not just in my own eyes, but in the way I carry myself forward. Give me the courage to step into what You are rebuilding without waiting until I feel worthy enough. Help me trust Your restoration more than I trust my regret. Amen.

Action Step

Write down one area where you have genuinely grown because of a past failure, not despite it, but through it. Thank God for the lesson, not for the shame, just the lesson. Then consider: what would it look like to let that growth count for something?

DAY 16
I Can Trust God with My Process

The Lie

"I should be further along by now."

So you measure. You compare timelines that were never meant to run parallel. You look at someone else's breakthrough and audit your own progress against it, and somehow, by that math, you always come up short.

The Truth in Christ

"He who began a good work in you will carry it on to completion."

In Christ, your process is not behind schedule, it is under His care. God does not start what He does not intend to finish.

Scripture Anchor

Philippians 1:6

Devotional

Comparison is one of the loudest voices in the healing process, and one of the least trustworthy.

It shows you someone else's visible breakthrough and says nothing about the years of quiet work that preceded it. It highlights their milestone and conceals their struggle. It hands you a measuring stick calibrated to someone else's journey and invites you to assess your own with it, which is a little like measuring your height against a ruler designed for a completely different frame.

The comparison was never fair. The timeline was never yours to begin with.

Healing is not linear. Growth unfolds in layers that do not always show on the surface. There are seasons when God is doing foundational work, strengthening what is underneath, stabilizing what has been shaken, quietly reinforcing what will eventually hold the weight of what is coming. That work is often invisible. It does not look like progress. It does not feel like movement. But it is some of the most essential work that happens in a person.

If frustration rises when you evaluate your progress, that makes sense. The culture around you rewards speed and visible results. Fast transformation makes compelling testimony. Slow, layered, quiet healing is harder to celebrate, but it is no less real, and no less led by God.

God is not anxious about your timeline. He is not checking a calendar and sighing. He is not disappointed in the days you feel tender or the seasons that feel repetitive. He is not grading your process, He is faithfully, unhurriedly completing it.

You are not behind. You are being formed. Those are not the same thing, and only one of them is true.

Renounce + Receive

I renounce: "I'm behind."

I receive: "God is faithfully completing His work in me."

Daily Affirmation

God is patient with my process, and so am I.

Prayer

Lord, quiet the comparison that makes my progress feel insufficient. Help me trust Your timing even when I cannot see what You are building. Anchor me in steady forward movement, not speed, not performance, just faithful presence with You in the process. Amen.

Action Step

The next time comparison shows up today, and it likely will, pause and say: "My process is personal. God is working here." Then let that be enough. Because today, it is.

DAY 17
I Am Not Weak — I Am Becoming Whole

The Lie

"My emotions mean I'm weak."

So you learned to hold it together. To stay composed when everything in you wanted to come undone. To measure your maturity by how unaffected you appeared, until numbness began to feel like an achievement and feeling anything at all started to feel like failure.

The Truth in Christ

"When I am weak, then I am strong."

In Christ, vulnerability is not weakness, it is the doorway to strength. God is not looking for people who have mastered the art of not feeling. He is looking for people willing to bring Him what is real.

Scripture Anchor

2 Corinthians 12:10

Devotional

There is a version of strength that is really just disciplined avoidance.

It looks composed. It looks mature. It holds everything together in public and falls apart quietly, alone, in the spaces where no one is watching. It equates silence with stability and tears with instability. It has learned to perform okayness so convincingly that sometimes even you believe it.

But numbness is not strength. It is protection. And for a season, that protection may have been necessary, a way of surviving what would have been too much to feel all at once. Your system did what it needed to do.

Healing, though, asks something different. It invites you to feel what you once had to set aside. That can be profoundly disorienting. Emotions that surface quickly, feel larger than the moment seems to warrant, or arrive without obvious triggers are not signs of instability. They are often signs that your system has finally reached a level of safety where it can begin processing what it stored. That is not regression. That is the work actually working.

God is not embarrassed by your emotions. He does not roll His eyes at your tears, grow impatient with your grief, or wish you would simply move on already. He meets you in what is real. He always has. The Psalms are full of people bringing God their unfiltered, unpolished, inconvenient emotional truth, and God meeting them there, not with correction, but with presence.

Strength in the Kingdom is not the ability to appear unaffected. It is the courage to bring what is real to the One who can actually do something with it.

Today, honesty wins over image.

Renounce + Receive

I renounce: "Feeling makes me weak."

I receive: "God strengthens me through honesty."

Daily Affirmation

I am becoming whole, not weak.

Prayer

Lord, help me stop treating my emotions like evidence against myself. Teach me to bring them to You unfiltered, not cleaned up, not minimized, not explained away. Strengthen me not by removing what I feel, but by meeting me within it. Amen.

Action Step

Name one emotion you have felt this week, just one, just honestly. Say it out loud: "This does not make me weak." Then sit with it for a moment instead of moving past it. Feeling it fully, even once, is its own kind of courage.

DAY 18
I Don't Have to Perform to Be Accepted

The Lie

"I'm only valuable when I'm useful."

So productivity became identity. Busyness became proof of worth. You learned to anticipate needs before they were spoken, to exceed expectations before anyone could be disappointed, to stay so indispensable that the thought of slowing down felt genuinely dangerous.

The Truth in Christ

"He has accepted us in the Beloved."

In Christ, you are accepted, not evaluated. Not assessed. Not conditionally approved pending next quarter's results. Accepted, fully, in Him.

Scripture Anchor

Ephesians 1:6

Devotional

Performance can become so second nature that you stop recognizing it as performance at all.

It just feels like responsibility. Like diligence. Like being the kind of person who shows up, follows through, and never lets anyone down. From the outside, it looks like strength. From the inside, it can feel like an engine that cannot find its off switch, always running, always producing, always staying one step ahead of the question: what happens if I stop?

That fear has a very specific answer it believes: if you stop producing, you stop mattering.

It is one of the most exhausting lies a person can carry, and it is remarkably good at disguising itself as virtue.

The anxiety that rises when you rest is worth paying attention to. The quiet voice that surfaces in stillness, telling you that you should be doing more, deserves examination. It may not be conviction. It may be conditioning. There is a significant difference between the Holy Spirit calling you to faithfulness and a wounded nervous system pulling you back into performance because performance once felt like safety.

God's acceptance is not productivity-based. He does not review your output before deciding how much affection to offer. He does not withhold presence until you have justified your existence for the day. You are not under evaluation. You are in relationship, and real relationships do not require you to continuously earn your place at the table.

You were accepted in Christ before you did a single thing to deserve it. That has not changed. It will not change, not on your most productive day, not on your most unproductive one.

Today, you exist without earning. That is not laziness. That is a clearer understanding of what grace actually means.

Renounce + Receive
I renounce: "I must perform to be valued."
I receive: "I am accepted in Christ."

Daily Affirmation
I am loved without performance.

Prayer

Father, quiet the relentless pressure to prove myself that lives just beneath the surface of everything I do. Teach me what it feels like to rest in Your acceptance without immediately looking for a way to earn it back. Break the performance patterns in me, gently, thoroughly, and at their root. Amen.

Action Step

Do one thing today slowly, without optimizing it, without doing it impressively, without making it count for something. Just do it at a human pace. Notice what comes up when you are not performing. That noticing is the work.

DAY 19
I Can Forgive Without Returning

The Lie

"If I forgive, I have to reconnect."

So forgiveness felt like a trap. Like the moment you released the resentment, you would be handing back the key to someone who had already proven what they would do with access. So you held on, not out of bitterness, but out of self-protection, because no one ever told you the two could be separated.

The Truth in Christ

"Leave room for God's justice."

In Christ, forgiveness releases your heart, not your boundaries. The outcome belongs to God. Your safety remains with you.

Scripture Anchor

Romans 12:19

Devotional

Forgiveness may be one of the most misunderstood teachings in the Christian faith, particularly for survivors.

It is often framed as reunion. As restoration of what was broken. As proof that healing has happened, evidenced by a willingness to return to proximity with the person who caused harm. And when you cannot do that, when your body says no before your theology can respond, shame sets in, as if the inability to reconcile means the forgiveness is not real.

But forgiveness and reconciliation are not the same thing. They have never been the same.

Forgiveness is a transaction between you and God. It is the decision to release the outcome, to stop carrying the weight of vengeance, to surrender the verdict to Someone with the authority and perspective to handle it rightly. It is an act of freedom, not for the person who harmed you, but for you. It unties you from the weight of what was done so you are no longer dragging it behind you.

Reconciliation is something else entirely. It requires safety. It requires demonstrated change. It requires the rebuilding of trust over time, and it is not always possible, not always wise, and not always what God asks.

You can forgive someone completely and never speak to them again. You can release resentment and still maintain a boundary. You can surrender vengeance to God and still protect what He is healing in you. These are not contradictions. They are wisdom operating as it should.

If the idea of forgiveness makes your chest tighten, pay attention to what that tension is telling you. It may be indicating that forgiveness has been used against you, weaponized to pressure you back into proximity with harm under the banner of obedience. That is not what God intended. His instruction to forgive was never meant to be a mechanism that keeps you unsafe.

Today, you release what you cannot control. And you keep what protects your peace.

Renounce + Receive

I renounce: "Forgiveness requires reconnection."

I receive: "God gives me wisdom and boundaries."

Daily Affirmation

I can forgive and still protect my peace.

Prayer

God, untangle the confusion around forgiveness that has made it feel like a threat rather than a gift. Help me release resentment without abandoning the wisdom that keeps me safe. Guard my heart with clarity, and help me trust You with the outcomes I cannot control. Amen.

Action Step

Sit quietly for a moment and ask yourself honestly: "What boundary is protecting my healing right now?" Name it. Honor it. A boundary that protects healing is not bitterness. It is stewardship.

DAY 20

I Can Grieve and Still Grow

The Lie

"If I grieve, I'll fall apart."

So the sorrow stayed packed away. Tucked behind productivity, behind service, behind the daily work of holding everything together. Because falling apart was not something you could afford, and grief, in your experience, had no guaranteed bottom.

The Truth in Christ

"Blessed are those who mourn, for they shall be comforted."

In Christ, grief is not regression, it is integration. Mourning is not the opposite of moving forward. Sometimes it is the only way through.

Scripture Anchor

Matthew 5:4

Devotional

There is a particular kind of exhaustion that comes from carrying grief you have never been given permission to set down.

It lives quietly in the body. In tightness that appears without warning. In emotion that surfaces at unexpected moments, a song, a smell, an ordinary Tuesday that suddenly brings sorrow you thought you had already handled. Grief has a way of finding the cracks in even the most carefully maintained composure.

And the fear underneath it all is this: if I start, I will not be able to stop.

That fear is understandable. When you have held yourself together for a long time, when stability has required constant effort, the idea of letting sorrow surface can feel genuinely dangerous. Like opening a door you cannot close again. Like choosing to come undone when coming undone is something you cannot afford.

But grief is not falling apart. It is evidence that something mattered.

The losses worth mourning are real. Lost time. Lost innocence. Lost trust. Lost versions of yourself that had to be set aside to survive. These are not small things to move past quickly. They are significant losses that deserve to be grieved, and if they never were, they are still waiting, patiently and persistently, for space to be honored.

God does not rush mourning. He does not stand at the edge of your sorrow with a timer, waiting for you to finish so you can return to being productive. He sits with you in it. He honors what was lost. He does not redeem grief by eliminating it, He redeems it by being present within it, and by restoring through it what only mourning can release.

Sorrow takes space. Giving it space is not weakness. It is the bravest kind of healing.

Renounce + Receive

I renounce: "Grieving means I'm stuck."
I receive: "God comforts me as I grow."

Daily Affirmation

I can grieve and still move forward.

Prayer

Lord, meet me in what I have lost, not to rush me through it, but to sit with me inside it. Comfort me at the pace my heart actually needs. Turn my mourning into strength, not by ending it prematurely, but by being faithful all the way through it. Amen.

Action Step

Open your journal to a blank page. Write about one loss, as much or as little as feels safe today. It does not have to be resolved. It does not have to lead anywhere. Just let it exist on the page instead of only inside you. That is enough. That is more than enough.

DAY 21
I Am Not Behind

The Lie

"I'm late. I missed my window."

So you do the math obsessively. You calculate what should have happened by now. You look at where others are and measure the distance between their milestones and your current place, and the gap begins to feel less like a difference in timing and more like evidence that something has gone permanently wrong.

The Truth in Christ

"He makes everything beautiful in its time."

In Christ, your timing is not wasted. What looks like delay to you has never once looked like delay to Him.

Scripture Anchor

Ecclesiastes 3:11

Devotional

Comparison is a thief with very specific taste, it takes time, the one thing you cannot earn back.

It shows you someone else's visible milestone and says nothing about the invisible years that preceded it. It shows you their arrival and hides their journey. It hands you a highlight reel edited to remove the struggle, the waiting, the seasons of quiet and unseen work, and then invites you to measure your unedited life against it.

That comparison was never fair. The conclusion it produces was never true.

There is a particular grief that comes with feeling like trauma stole time that cannot be recovered. Years spent surviving instead of thriving. Seasons lost to healing that others seemed to spend building. It is a real loss, and it deserves to be acknowledged. But grief over lost time is different from the belief that the window has permanently closed, and trauma has a way of collapsing that distinction until they feel the same.

They are not the same.

God redeems timelines. Not by turning back clocks or pretending the lost seasons did not cost anything, but by working so thoroughly in what remains that the math begins to break in the most beautiful way. What feels delayed may actually be depth being built. What feels slow may be foundational work happening beneath the surface, work the visible structure will one day depend on entirely.

Urgency is not the same as calling. Anxiety is not prophecy. The panic that says hurry, you are running out of time is not the voice of God. It is the voice of a nervous system that has learned to treat stillness as danger and waiting as abandonment.

You are not behind. You are being prepared. And there is a difference.

Renounce + Receive

I renounce: "I'm behind."

I receive: "God's timing is intentional."

Daily Affirmation

I am right on time in God's hands.

Prayer

Father, release me from the pressure of timelines I was never meant to keep. Quiet the comparison that makes Your pacing feel like neglect. Anchor me in purpose instead of panic, and help me trust that what You are doing in the waiting is as intentional as what You will do when the waiting ends. Amen.

Action Step

Identify one comparison trigger, an account, a conversation, a habit, that consistently makes you feel behind. Remove it, mute it, or step back from it today, even temporarily. Protecting your perspective is not avoidance. It is wisdom.

DAY 22
I Am Not Stuck

The Lie

"Nothing will change."

So effort starts to feel pointless. You do the work, show up to the process, choose the harder and healthier path, and then look around and find everything apparently unchanged. The lie does not need to argue. It simply points to the evidence and lets the exhaustion speak for itself.

The Truth in Christ

"See, I am doing a new thing."

In Christ, progress may be quiet, but it is happening. God does not announce every move He makes before He makes it. He simply works.

Scripture Anchor

Isaiah 43:19

Devotional

Stuck is one of the heaviest feelings in the healing process, because it does not just describe where you are. It predicts where you are going.

Nothing will change is not a neutral observation. It is a verdict. And once that verdict settles in, it begins to color everything. Effort feels futile. The work feels performative. Hope feels naive. Why keep choosing differently if differently never seems to lead anywhere new?

But here is what that feeling consistently gets wrong: growth is almost always invisible before it becomes visible.

There are seasons when nothing looks different on the surface, and everything is shifting underneath. Reactions that once hijacked you entirely now only slow you down for a moment. Boundaries that once felt impossible are becoming more natural. Thoughts that once felt like facts now feel more like visitors you can observe rather than residents you must obey. These are not small changes. They are the internal renovations that precede every meaningful external transformation.

The challenge is that internal change does not photograph well. It does not produce milestones you can point to. It rarely feels like progress while it is happening. It becomes visible in retrospect, when you look back and realize you are not who you were, even if you cannot name the exact moment things shifted.

God does not despise gradual transformation. He is not waiting for your breakthrough to be dramatic enough to count. He is present in the quiet shifts, the softened reactions, the boundary held once when it would not have been before, the moment you caught the lie before it finished its sentence.

That counts. All of it counts.

Today, you look for subtle evidence of growth, not to convince yourself healing is real, but because it is, and you deserve to see it.

Renounce + Receive

I renounce: "I'll always be this way."

I receive: "God is making a way forward."

Daily Affirmation

Change is happening in me.

Prayer

Lord, help me see the progress I have been too discouraged to notice. Strengthen my patience with a process that moves at its own pace. Remind me that You are always working, even in seasons that feel silent, even on days that feel identical to the ones before. Amen.

Action Step

Write down one small change you have noticed in yourself this year. Not a milestone. Not a breakthrough. Just one quiet shift that would have been impossible before. Find it. Write it down. Let it be evidence. Because it is.

DAY 23
I Can Start Again

The Lie

"It's too late to begin again."

So the thing stays paused. The dream stays shelved. The step you almost took remains untaken, because failure has a way of turning temporary setbacks into permanent conclusions, and shame is quick to agree.

The Truth in Christ

"His mercies are new every morning."

In Christ, you are never beyond restoration. Every morning that arrives is God's answer to the lie that your chance has passed.

Scripture Anchor

Lamentations 3:22–23

Devotional

Failure is a convincing storyteller.

It takes one chapter, or several, and writes an ending. It tells you the opportunity has passed, the damage is done, the door that once stood open has closed permanently in the time you spent not being ready. It speaks with such authority that questioning it can feel foolish. Of course it is too late. Look at the evidence.

But failure is not a prophet. It is a wound speaking.

Every morning that arrives, unremarkable, ordinary, another day that looks like the ones before it, is a quiet theological statement. Mercy is new. Not recycled from yesterday, not rationed based on recent performance, not conditional on whether you have earned another attempt. New. Fresh. Available before you have done a single thing to deserve it.

Starting again is not the same as failing again. That distinction matters more than it might feel right now.

There is real humility in beginning again, in acknowledging the last attempt did not go as planned and choosing to try again anyway. That is not the posture of someone who has learned nothing. It is the posture of someone who has learned the most important thing: the alternative to starting again is staying exactly where you are, which was never what you were made for.

Shame will tell you that trying again is naive. That you should know better by now. That the desire to begin is simply setting you up for the same disappointment again. But shame is not your shepherd. It does not have your best interests at its center. It does not lead you anywhere worth going.

God does.

And every morning He offers the same quiet evidence: you are still here. The mercy is still new. You are not done.

Today, beginning wins over hiding.

Renounce + Receive

I renounce: "It's too late."

I receive: "God gives me fresh starts."

Daily Affirmation

I am allowed to begin again.

Prayer

God, quiet the voice that has convinced me the window is closed. Give me the courage to take the next step toward something I have been too afraid to return to. Thank You that Your mercies do not keep score, and that today is evidence I am not finished. Amen.

Action Step

Identify one thing you have paused, a goal, a practice, your connection with God, a dream. Take one small step toward it today. Not a full return. Just one step. Beginning does not require momentum. It only requires willingness. Start there.

DAY 24

I Am Not Defined by What Was Done to Me

The Lie

"What was done to me defines me."

So the wound became the lens. Every relationship filtered through it. Every opportunity assessed by it. Every version of the future imagined with it at the center, not as something that happened, but as something that determined what was possible from here.

The Truth in Christ

"To bestow on them a crown of beauty instead of ashes..."

In Christ, you are not defined by devastation, you are marked by restoration. God does not look at what was done to you and call it your identity. He looks at what He is doing in you and calls it your future.

Scripture Anchor

Isaiah 61:3

Devotional

There is a difference between acknowledging trauma and being named by it, but trauma works hard to collapse that distinction.

It does not happen all at once. It happens gradually, the way water shapes stone, slowly and consistently, until the shape feels so natural you forget it was ever different. What began as a wound becomes a filter. The filter becomes a framework. The framework becomes an identity so deeply internalized that imagining yourself outside of it feels not only difficult but somehow dishonest, as if releasing it would mean pretending it never happened.

But acknowledging what happened and being defined by it are not the same act. One is truth-telling. The other is a sentence trauma has no authority to declare.

Ashes are not identity. They are material.

And what God does with material, especially the kind that has been through fire, is never insignificant. Isaiah 61 is not a poem about denying devastation. It is a declaration of what happens after it. The ashes are real. The mourning is real. The grief is honored in full. And then, not instead of all that, but through it, God crowns. He exchanges. He builds something from the rubble that could not have existed without it.

Trauma wires the brain to anticipate repetition. If harm came from a certain direction before, the nervous system prepares for it to come again. That is not a character flaw, it is a protection mechanism doing its job. But protection mechanisms were never meant to write your future. They were meant to keep you alive long enough to have one.

Redemption interrupts repetition. Not by erasing the past, but by refusing to let it author what comes next.

God does not waste suffering. But He does not let it have the final word either.

Today, you separate your story from your identity and hand the pen back to the One who writes endings worth reading.

Renounce + Receive
I renounce: "My trauma defines me."
I receive: "God defines my identity and my future."

Daily Affirmation

I am defined by God's redemption, not my wounds.

Prayer

Lord, rewrite the narrative I absorbed without realizing it, the one that made what happened to me the most important thing about me. Help me see myself the way You do, beyond the wound and into restoration. Crown what has been through fire with something only You could create from it. Amen.

Action Step

Write this sentence somewhere you will see it: "What happened to me is part of my story, not my identity." Read it once as a statement. Then read it again as a declaration. Notice the difference.

DAY 25
I Am Not a Burden

The Lie

"I am too much for people."

So you learned to need less and carry more. To say I'm fine with enough conviction that people stopped asking, which, if you are honest, was exactly what you hoped for. Because needing something and having that need met with frustration taught you a lasting lesson: wanting things from people is dangerous.

The Truth in Christ

"Cast all your anxiety on Him because He cares for you."

In Christ, your needs are not irritating, they are welcomed. Not tolerated. Not managed. Welcomed.

Scripture Anchor

1 Peter 5:7

Devotional

When needs are consistently met with frustration, silence, or overwhelm, the lesson is absorbed quickly and deeply: you are too much.

It does not have to be taught directly. It shows up in the sigh before the response. In the shift in the room when you asked for something. In the pattern of reaching out and finding people either unavailable or burdened by your reaching. Over time, you stopped reaching. You learned to manage alone. You built a version of yourself that required very little from anyone and called it strength, because the alternative was admitting how much it cost you.

But having needs is not the same as being a burden. That distinction matters.

Every human being who has ever lived has had needs, physical, emotional, relational, spiritual. Needing is not a character flaw. It is evidence of being human. The people who taught you that your needs were too much were not telling you the truth about your needs. They were revealing the limits of their own capacity. Those are not the same, and you were never meant to carry the confusion between them.

God does not sigh when you come to Him. He does not check how recently you last asked before deciding whether to be present. He does not grow impatient with your process or keep a quiet tally of how many times you have needed the same thing. He does not make you feel foolish for returning to the same fear, the same struggle, the same prayer you have prayed a hundred times before.

He invites it. All of it. Every time.

If guilt rises when you think about asking for support, from God or from safe people, pause before accepting that guilt as truth. It may not be truth. It may be old conditioning presenting itself as self-awareness. There is a difference between conviction that leads to growth and shame that keeps you small, silent, and alone.

Today, you bring your needs into the light. First to God, who already knows them. Then, slowly and wisely, to the safe people He has placed around you.

You are not too much. You were simply in rooms too small to hold you.

Renounce + Receive

I renounce: "I am a burden."

I receive: "God cares deeply about me."

Daily Affirmation

I am worthy of care and compassion.

Prayer

Father, heal the shame that formed around my needs in seasons when they were treated as inconveniences. Teach me, slowly and patiently, that I am not too much for You. Surround me with people safe enough to practice asking, and give me the courage to let them help. Amen.

Action Step

Ask for one small thing today, from God or from a safe person in your life. It does not have to be significant. It just has to be real. Notice the discomfort of asking, and ask anyway. That is not weakness. That is your nervous system learning something new.

DAY 26
My Needs Matter

The Lie

"My needs don't matter."

So you stopped voicing them. You hinted instead of asked. You waited to see whether someone would notice, and when they didn't, you quietly filed it away as confirmation: nobody is really paying attention, and bringing it up would only make things uncomfortable. Better to need nothing. Better to be easy.

The Truth in Christ

"My God will meet all your needs according to the riches of His glory."

In Christ, your needs are not selfish, they are human. God does not promise to meet what does not exist. The promise itself assumes the needs are real.

Scripture Anchor

Philippians 4:19

Devotional

There is a kind of praise that sounds like a compliment and functions like a cage.

She's so low-maintenance. So easy. Never asks for anything. In certain environments, this was the highest compliment you could receive, to be the person who required the least, adapted the most, and kept everyone comfortable by making yourself as small and uncomplicated as possible.

And you learned to wear it like a virtue. Because the alternative, having needs, voicing them, asking directly for what you required, had not gone well before. Requests had been met with frustration. Needs had been treated as inconveniences. So you stopped requesting. You started hinting, hoping, waiting, and then quietly absorbing the disappointment when no one picked up on what you never actually said.

But unspoken needs do not disappear. They go underground. And underground, they do not stay still. They leak. They surface as resentment toward people who never knew what you needed. As exhaustion from carrying things you were never meant to carry alone. As shutdown when the accumulation becomes more than your system can quietly contain.

Clarity is not confrontation. That distinction is worth sitting with.

Asking directly for what you need is not aggression. It is not selfishness. It is not making yourself a burden. It is giving the people in your life the information they need to actually show up for you, which is something hinting can never do. Hinting is asking while also protecting yourself from the vulnerability of having asked. It shields you from the direct experience of rejection, but it also shields you from the direct experience of being genuinely known and met.

Healing includes learning to say the sentence all the way to the end. I need this. That didn't feel okay. It would help me if. These are not demands. They are the language of someone who has decided their inner life is worth communicating, and that the people worth keeping in their life can handle hearing it.

Your needs are not too specific, too frequent, or too inconvenient to matter. They are simply yours. And they are worthy of a voice.

Renounce + Receive

I renounce: "My needs don't matter."

I receive: "God cares about what I need."

Daily Affirmation

My needs are valid and worthy of being voiced.

Prayer

God, give me the courage to say what is true without softening it into something unrecognizable. Help me communicate with calm and clarity, not from fear, not from demand, but from the quiet confidence that my needs are worth naming. Heal the part of me that still believes silence is safer than honesty. Amen.

Action Step

Write one clear, complete sentence: "I need ______." Do not hint at it. Do not soften it. Write the whole thing. Then decide where it belongs, in prayer, conversation, or boundary. And take one step toward putting it there.

DAY 27
I Can Be Loved and Still Be Wise

The Lie

"Love requires ignoring red flags."

So you talked yourself out of what you noticed. You labeled your instincts as anxiety, your caution as jadedness, your hesitation as fear of intimacy. You told yourself that a person who had healed enough would be able to trust, and so the discomfort you felt became evidence against yourself rather than information worth taking seriously.

The Truth in Christ

"If any of you lacks wisdom, let him ask of God..."

In Christ, love and discernment work together. They were never meant to compete. God does not ask you to choose between an open heart and a clear mind.

Scripture Anchor

James 1:5

Devotional

When longing for connection has been strong enough and long enough, the temptation to override intuition can feel almost reasonable.

You want this to work. You want this person to be safe. You want the version of the relationship that exists in the hopeful part of your imagination, and the signal your body is sending feels like an obstacle between you and that hope. So you negotiate with it. You find explanations for what concerned you. You remind yourself that you have been wrong before, that you tend to overthink, that not everyone who makes you uncomfortable is actually dangerous.

Sometimes that self-correction is healthy. Sometimes what feels like a red flag is old fear responding to a trigger that has little to do with the current person or situation. Discernment includes knowing the difference.

But there is another kind of override, the kind that happens not because you have genuinely assessed the situation, but because you do not want the discomfort to mean what it seems to mean. The kind where you silence your instincts not through wisdom but through longing. And that kind of override has a cost that compounds over time.

Discernment is not paranoia. It is not the voice of someone too wounded to trust. It is wisdom, specifically the kind of wisdom sharpened, not dulled, by experience. What you have been through has not only left you with wounds. It has also left you with a finely tuned ability to read rooms, relationships, and patterns others might miss. That is not damage. That is data.

God does not require blindness as the price of love. He does not ask you to ignore what He built into you in order to be in relationship. He invites clarity, not suspicion, not cynicism, but clear-eyed, wisdom-rooted, discernment-led engagement with the people He places in your life.

Your body often knows before your mind is willing to admit it. When something knots in your stomach, when something feels slightly off, when the story someone tells does not quite add up, that signal is worth pausing over. Not panicking over. Not acting on impulsively. But pausing over. Praying over. Taking seriously enough to examine before dismissing.

Love and wisdom have always belonged together. Today, you refuse to choose between them.

Renounce + Receive

I renounce: "Wisdom ruins love."

I receive: "God gives me discernment."

Daily Affirmation

I love with clarity and wisdom.

Prayer

Lord, sharpen the discernment You have built into me, and help me trust it without shame. Teach me to honor the signals You have given me rather than negotiating them away because connection feels more urgent than caution. Protect my heart with wisdom, and help me love well because of it, not in spite of it. Amen.

Action Step

If something feels off today, in a relationship, a conversation, or a situation, resist the reflex to explain it away immediately. Pause. Pray. Give it a moment before deciding what it means. Your instincts are not your enemy. They may be exactly what God is using to guide you.

DAY 28
I Am Free to Obey God

The Lie

"Obedience will cost me safety."

So you kept a careful distance from surrender. You engaged with faith on your own terms, close enough to believe, cautious enough to never fully let go. Because the people who had asked for your obedience before had not proven trustworthy with it. And somewhere in that wound, God was included in the verdict.

The Truth in Christ

"I came that they may have life, and have it abundantly."

In Christ, obedience leads toward life, not away from it. God's direction has never been designed to diminish you. It has always been oriented toward your flourishing.

Scripture Anchor

John 10:10

Devotional

Few things complicate faith more deeply than having authority misused against you in God's name.

When obedience has been weaponized, used to silence your questions, control your choices, or keep you in proximity to harm under the banner of submission, the word itself becomes loaded. It carries the weight of every time compliance was demanded rather than invited, every time your hesitation was labeled rebellion, every time someone used spiritual language to override your instincts and called it discipleship.

That was not God. That was people misusing His name and His design.

God does not manipulate through fear. He does not manufacture urgency to pressure you past your own discernment. He does not use spiritual language to override your instincts or demand compliance as proof of devotion. His voice does not sound like coercion. It does not leave you feeling smaller, more confused, or more trapped than before you heard it.

His voice is steady. Convicting, yes, but conviction and coercion are not the same. Conviction moves toward something. It clarifies. It opens. It brings a quality of peace even when what it asks requires courage. Coercion, by contrast, closes. It pressures. It produces anxiety, confusion, and the quiet sense that you do not have a real choice.

Learning to separate God's guidance from the misuse of human authority is slow, necessary work. It requires sitting with Scripture long enough to see how Jesus actually led people, with invitation, not ultimatum. With truth, not manipulation. With a consistent orientation toward life, freedom, wholeness, and dignity.

If obedience makes your chest tighten, that response deserves examination rather than dismissal. Ask honestly: is this the fear of someone harmed by counterfeit authority, or the wisdom of someone recognizing genuine danger? Those are different responses, requiring different answers. God is patient enough to help you discern which one it is.

What He is leading you toward has always been life. Not performance. Not diminishment. Not fear dressed up as faithfulness. Life, abundant and oriented toward wholeness. That is what obedience to Him has always been for.

Renounce + Receive

I renounce: "God's will is unsafe."

I receive: "God leads me into life."

Daily Affirmation

I trust God's leadership in my life.

Prayer

Father, untangle the fear that formed around obedience when authority was misused against me. Help me hear Your voice clearly, steady, convicting, and consistently oriented toward my flourishing. Lead me toward life and freedom, and help me trust that those are always where You are taking me. Amen.

Action Step

Ask God one simple, honest question today, something you have been holding or avoiding. Then sit quietly for a minute. Not to manufacture an answer, but to practice listening. Obedience begins with learning whose voice is worth following. Start by giving His voice room.

DAY 29
My Story Will Not End in Shame

The Lie

"My story is ruined."

So you stopped imagining how it ends. Every time you tried, the broken chapters surfaced before the hopeful ones. Shame argued that what has already been written is more determinative than what has not been written yet. The conclusion felt settled before the story was finished.

The Truth in Christ

"I will repay you for the years the locusts have eaten."

In Christ, restoration outruns regret. God does not enter a story to assess the damage and walk away. He enters it to rewrite the outcome, and He has never been intimidated by the chapter He walked into.

Scripture Anchor

Joel 2:25

Devotional

Shame is a very specific kind of liar. It does not just tell you that you did something wrong, it tells you that what went wrong has permanently determined what comes next.

It takes the broken chapters and holds them up as evidence of the ending. It argues that certain seasons disqualify the whole book, that the damage is too extensive, too visible, too woven into the narrative to be redeemed without remainder. And it delivers this verdict with such quiet certainty that questioning it can feel naive, like insisting on hope when the evidence seems otherwise.

But shame is not a narrator. It is a wound speaking beyond its authority.

The promise in Joel 2 is one of the most audacious in Scripture, not because it minimizes what the locusts took, but because it refuses to let them have the final account. The years are acknowledged. The loss is named. God does not wave it away or pretend the devastation was less than it was. He looks at the full extent of what was consumed and says, I will repay. Not partially. Not symbolically. Repay.

This is not a minor theological detail. It directly challenges every conclusion shame has drawn about your story. Redemption does not work by editing out difficult chapters. It works by entering them fully, without flinching, and refusing to let them be the last word. God is not a distant editor marking up your manuscript from afar. He is a co-author who stepped into the story, into its hardest parts, and began writing forward from exactly where things broke.

If regret or embarrassment still rises when you revisit certain seasons, that makes sense. Memory is not linear. Healing is not the absence of feeling. But the presence of shame is not proof that shame is right. It is evidence that the wound is still tender, not that the verdict is final.

Your story is not over. The ending has not been written. And the Author has never lost a narrative He chose to redeem.

Shame does not get the last word here. It never did.

Renounce + Receive

I renounce: "My story ends in shame."

I receive: "God is redeeming my story."

Daily Affirmation

My story is being restored.

Prayer

God, heal the regret that surfaces when I revisit certain chapters, not by removing the memory, but by changing what it means. Redeem what feels permanently lost. Write an ending over my life that only You could author, one marked not by what was broken, but by what You restored from it. Amen.

Action Step

Write one sentence, just one, that begins with these words: "My story is not over because..." Let it be true. Let it be yours. Then read it back to yourself slowly. That sentence is shame's eviction notice. Let it land.

DAY 30
I Will Live Renewed

The Lie

"Change won't last."

So you held your progress at arm's length. You allowed yourself a little hope, but not fully, because you have been here before. The breakthrough that did not hold. The clarity that eventually faded. The version of yourself you worked so hard to become, undone by one difficult week, or so it seemed. So you learned to celebrate quietly, cautiously, with one eye already watching for regression.

The Truth in Christ

"Be transformed by the renewing of your mind."

In Christ, renewal is not a moment you arrive at and then defend. It is a practice you return to, daily, deliberately, and with increasing confidence over time.

Scripture Anchor

Romans 12:2

Devotional

This is not a finish line. It never was.

Thirty days ago, you began practicing something, the practice of noticing lies, naming them, and refusing to let them run unchallenged through your mind. That practice does not expire today. It does not reset or disappear because the calendar moved past Day 30. What you have been building is not temporary. It is a skill, and skills, once learned, become part of who you are.

You are not who you were when you began. That may be hard to see from the inside, where change is slower and less dramatic than it appears in retrospect. But something has shifted. In the way you recognize a lie before it finishes its sentence. In the way you pause where you once spiraled. In the way truth has begun to feel less like an argument and more like something you actually believe, at least some of the time, on the better days.

That is not nothing. That is everything.

Freedom is not the permanent absence of old thoughts. If you are waiting for the day familiar lies stop appearing entirely, you may be waiting for something that is not the point. Freedom is the ability to recognize what arrives, to see the thought for what it is, to refuse to partner with it, and to reach for truth with a steadiness that grows stronger with practice. That is what renewal looks like from the inside. Less dramatic than expected. More durable than you feared.

And this changes everything: this was never only about you.

God restores survivors, and then He raises leaders. The healing you have done over these 30 days has always carried a reach beyond your own life. Your steadiness will become someone else's safety. Your clarity will become someone else's permission to pursue their own. Your willingness to name the lie, hold the boundary, receive love, grieve loss, begin again, all of it creates a kind of permission in others that nothing else can.

You did not go through what you went through so the story would end with you.

You went through it so that what God did in you could become a door for someone else.

Today is not an ending. It is a commissioning. You leave these 30 days not with a certificate of completion, but with a practice, a posture, and a purpose, along with the full weight of what God has begun in you, which He has already promised to complete.

Go. Lead from healing. Live renewed. The world needs exactly what you have become.

Renounce + Receive

I renounce: "Change won't last."

I receive: "God is renewing me daily."

Daily Affirmation

I live renewed, and I lead from healing.

Prayer

Lord, seal what You have begun in these 30 days, not as a conclusion, but as a foundation. Help me return to truth daily, even when returning feels like starting over. Use my healing to create safety for those around me. Let what You restored in me become a door someone else can walk through. Amen.

Action Step

Before you close this book today, write down one concrete shift you have experienced in these 30 days. Not a goal. Not an aspiration. Something already true that was not, or not as true, when you began. Hold it. Name it. Thank God for it. Then carry it forward as evidence, for yourself on the harder days ahead, that change is real, that it lasts, and that God finishes what He starts. You are the proof.

CONCLUSION
Keep Renewing — Keep Becoming

You made it to the end of this book. But you have not reached the end of this journey, because this journey does not end. It has a direction. And today, you are more oriented in that direction than you were 30 days ago.

That matters more than it may feel right now.

Renewal is not a finish line. It is a returning, the daily, deliberate practice of coming back to truth when the lies get loud again. And they will get loud again. Not because you failed. Not because the healing was not real. But because this is how the mind works. Old wiring does not disappear the moment new wiring is formed. It fades gradually, losing authority one decision at a time, as you continue choosing truth over what once felt like fact.

Freedom is not the permanent absence of old thoughts. It is the ability to recognize them, to see the lie before it finishes its sentence, to name what is happening in your nervous system without being governed by it, to reach for truth not because it feels easier, but because you have practiced reaching for it long enough that it has become instinct. That is what these 30 days have been building. Not a feeling. A practice. And practices, unlike feelings, remain when circumstances get hard.

You are not who you were when you opened this book. You may not see that clearly yet. Change is always more visible in retrospect than in real time. But something has shifted. In the way you recognize a lie. In the way you pause before you spiral. In the way truth has begun to feel less like an argument and more like something you actually believe, at least on the better days, at least more than before.

Hold that. It is evidence. And on the days when old voices grow loud and old patterns feel closer than you would like, you will need that evidence.

Here is what is also true: God does not waste pain. He does not waste the years that felt lost, the seasons that cost more than they should have, or the chapters you would have written differently if you had the choice. He redeems what He did not author. He enters the places of deepest damage and builds from them something that could not have existed without them, wisdom that is specific, compassion that is earned, steadiness that was forged rather than borrowed.

You are not just healing. You are being formed. And what God forms in a person is never only for that person.

Your steadiness will become someone else's safety. Your clarity will give someone else permission to pursue their own. Your willingness to name the lie, hold the boundary, receive love, grieve loss, and begin again creates a kind of permission in the people watching you that nothing else can. Survivors who become whole do not just recover. They lead. They create spaces where others finally feel safe enough to begin.

That is what your healing has always been moving toward.

So keep renewing. Not because you have not done enough, but because renewal is not a destination. It is the most honest description of what a transformed life looks like from the inside. It is the daily return. The ongoing choice. The practice that becomes, over time, the most natural part of you.

Renewal is no longer something you read about. It is something you live. It is something you are.

And the world needs exactly what you have become.

About the Author

Alicia Baker knows what it means to need a book like this, because she has lived the kind of life that made it necessary.

After years of surviving trauma, addiction, and human trafficking, Alicia encountered the life-changing grace of Jesus Christ. That encounter did not just save her life. It reoriented it completely, shifting her from survival mode into something she had never known before: purpose.

Today, she walks alongside women and families as a faith-driven life coach, reentry case manager, speaker, and author. Her work sits at the intersection of Christ-centered healing, trauma-informed care, and practical restoration. It is shaped at every level by an understanding that comes only from having lived it. She does not lead from theory. She leads from testimony.

Alicia is passionate about one thing above all: helping people separate lies from truth. The lie that says your past defines you. The lie that says you have gone too far. The lie that says this is just who you are now. She has lived inside those lies. She knows their texture, their logic, their convincing weight. And she knows, from both personal experience and professional practice, that they are not the final word.

Through coaching, speaking, writing, and community outreach, she carries a message that is both simple and unrelenting: no one is too far gone for God's love. Healing is possible. Freedom is real. And purpose waits on the other side of surrender.

Alicia believes, with everything she has, that survivors do not just recover. They lead. And she is living proof.

You don't have to walk your healing journey alone.

If this devotional spoke to you...

If you saw yourself in these pages...

If you're ready to go deeper than awareness into true transformation...

Then this is your next step.

At **Crowned Jewels Life Coaching**, we help women move from **brokenness to wholeness**—through Christ-centered healing, identity restoration, and practical transformation.

Take Your Next Step:

Your healing didn't end with this book...

This is just the beginning.

Visit: www.mycrownedjewels.com

Apply for Coaching or Book a Discovery Call

You are not too broken.

You are not too far gone.

You are not disqualified.

You are a Crowned Jewel. 💎

And your healing is worth investing in.

www.ingramcontent.com/pod-product-compliance
Lightning Source LLC
LaVergne TN
LVHW090616110826
845146LV00001B/413
* 9 7 9 8 9 9 5 3 7 4 1 9 0 *